Canada /
971 MEI   32070003650152

Meister, Cari.
ARMOUR ELEMENTARY SCHOOL

Y0-CFU-517

	DATE DUE		

971   Meister, Cari.
MEI   Canada

Armour Elementary School
Chicago Public Schools
950 W 33rd Pl
Chicago, IL 60608

Going Places

Canada

Cari Meister
ABDO Publishing Company

visit us at
www.abdopub.com

Published by ABDO Publishing Company 4940 Viking Drive, Edina, Minnesota 55435. Copyright © 2000 by Abdo Consulting Group, Inc. International copyrights reserved in all countries. No part of this book may be reproduced in any form without written permission from the publisher.

Printed in the United States.

Photo credits: Peter Arnold, Inc., SuperStock

Edited by Lori Kinstad Pupeza
Contributing editor Morgan Hughes
Graphic designs by Linda O'Leary

Library of Congress Cataloging-in-Publication Data

Meister, Cari.
    Canada / Cari Meister.
    p. cm. -- (Going places)
    Includes index.
    Summary: Describes a variety of tourist attractions found in one of the largest countries in the world, including mountains, lakes, national parks, cities, festivals, and outdoor activities, such as tobogganing, mushing, and panning for gold.
    ISBN 1-57765-028-X
    1. Canada--Juvenile literature. [1. Canada.] I. Title. II. Series: Meister, Cari. Going places.
F1008.2.M45 2000
971--dc21   98-10139
                                                                                                 CIP
                                                                                                 AC

Contents

Visiting Canada 4
Canada's Native People 6
National Parks 8
Forts 10
Making Money 12
In Search of Polar Bears 14
Panning for Gold 16
Mushing 18
More Outdoor Fun 20
Glossary 22
Internet Sites 23
Index 24

Visiting Canada

*T*all mountains, clear lakes, busy cities, and **native** festivals draw many people to Canada every year. Canada is a place for adventure. There are lots of things to do and see.

Canada is one of the largest countries in the world. Canada is located north of the United States. Canada reaches very far north. It almost touches the North Pole! Canada is divided into provinces and territories. Provinces and territories are like states. Canada has ten provinces and two territories.

Most **Canadians** live near cities. Major cities like Montreal, Quebec, Toronto, and Vancouver have theaters, museums, and parks. Many parts of Canada are **undeveloped**. If you like to explore the outdoors, you'll love Canada.

Banff National Park, Alberta, Canada.

This map shows the territories and provinces of Canada.

Canada's Native People

There were groups of people living in Canada for thousands of years before the **Europeans** arrived and built their first settlement in 1605. These people are called **native**, because they were the first people to live in Canada.

Inuits, sometimes called Eskimos, also lived in Canada before Europeans arrived. The Inuits lived very far north, where it is cold.

Today there are about 375,000 native and Inuit people living in Canada. Many of their ways have changed. Some of their ways have stayed the same. Some native and Inuit people live like their **ancestors** did.

There are many ways to learn about the Inuit and native people of Canada. You can visit a native or Inuit museum, village, or reservation. There are many open to the public throughout the country. At Ksan Native Village in British Columbia you can see the highest totem pole in the world.

An Inuit child dressed in a traditional parka.

National Parks

There are over 80 national parks and historical sites in Canada. Because Canada is so big, it covers many different kinds of land. Some national parks have mountains, lakes, and trees. Other national parks are on the ocean's rocky coasts. In the north, you would see **tundra**.

There are many things to do at a national park. You can hike, bike, or sightsee. You can camp, swim, or ski. At some parks, like Jasper National Park in Alberta, you can ride a **gondola**. At Banff National Park, you can ride in a Snocoach across the Rocky Mountain's largest icefield. At Gros Morne National Park, you can see majestic **fjords** that cut into the Atlantic Ocean.

While at a national park you can also listen and look for wildlife. Bighorn sheep, bears, wolves, lynx, fish, moose, and many other animals live in Canada.

A hiker enjoys the scenic view of this waterfall in Alberta, Canada.

Forts

You can learn a lot about the way people lived in the past by visiting a fort. There are forts all over Canada. At some of the forts there are museums. At other forts, people in costumes act out the past.

In Nova Scotia, at the Fortress of Louisbourg, people speak French. They wear French clothes and make French food. Louisbourg was a French city inside a fort. Today in Canada French is the second most widely spoken language after English. It is the official language of Quebec.

At Fort Walsh National Park in Saskatchewan, you can watch men and women in red coats act out scenes from a Mountie's life. Mounties were like sheriffs of the Old West. They rode on horseback into the Canadian countryside to bring order.

There are still Mounties today. They're called the Royal Canadian Mounted Police. Although, they rarely mount a horse. Today they drive cars or motorcycles.

Fortress of Louisbourg in Nova Scotia, Canada.

Making Money

You can watch money being made at the Royal Canadian Mint. The Royal Canadian Mint is located in Winnipeg, Manitoba. On a tour, you can see money coming out of machines. Watch workers put hundreds of dollars worth of coins into plastic bags! The bags of money are shipped off to places in Canada and other parts of the world.

The Canadian Mint makes all of Canada's coins. They also make coins for other countries. The Canadian Mint makes coins for Australia, Figi, New Zealand, Bangladesh, and Tanzania.

Canadian money is very much like American money. There are pennies, nickels, dimes, quarters, and dollars. In the United States, $1 comes in a paper bill and a coin. In Canada there is only a $1 coin. There is a picture of a loon on one side of the Canadian dollar coin. **Canadians** call these coins "loonies."

Newly minted Canadian quarters.

In Search of Polar Bears

There's a place on the Hudson Bay where you can watch polar bears. Churchill, a rugged outpost located in Manitoba, is right in the middle of a major arctic **migration** route.

Between June and September many people come to watch the 3,000 beluga whales swimming through the area. People also come to see the polar bears.

Churchill's polar bears start to come ashore when the ice on Hudson Bay starts to break. The polar bears stay in Churchill until early November. This is usually when the ice starts to refreeze. The best polar bear sightings are in September and October.

You can see the polar bears by boat, helicopter, or by **tundra** buggy. There are many guides in Churchill.

Polar Bears are fascinating creatures. They are big and white. They look cuddly. Don't be fooled! Polar Bears are very dangerous animals.

Three polar bears near Hudson Bay, Canada.

Panning for Gold

In the 1880s, people rushed to the Klondike River in search of gold. Over one million people left home and headed to the Yukon Territory in hopes of striking it rich.

Big towns were built. Saloons, restaurants, and lodges sprung up in the middle of the wilderness. Only about 4,000 people found gold. After a while, **prospectors** left. The towns became deserted.

Today you can visit Dawson. Dawson is an old deserted mining town. There is an old theater, church, store, gambling house, and the Canadian Bank of Commerce. Miners had their gold weighed at the Canadian Bank of Commerce.

A gold panning competition in Dawson, Canada.

Mushing

Mushing is only for people who love wild adventures. You also have to enjoy hard work, cold weather, and demanding dogs.

Mushing means to travel by dogsled. Canada is a perfect place to dogsled. There is a lot of snow and pretty land. There is a lot of open space.

Wells Gray Ranch in British Columbia offers three-day and five-day musher adventures. On these trips a person can mush every day. The dogs pull you over old logging roads, by lakes, and up and down mountain ridges. Try to keep the snow spray out of your eyes! There are many beautiful things to see.

One, two, three . . . mush! Hang on! Dogs run fast. You can travel up to 30 miles (48 km) in one day!

A musher and her dog team.

More Outdoor Fun

*T*here are hundreds of other outdoor things to do in Canada. Because most of Canada has a long winter, many **Canadians** enjoy winter sports. In Canada there are thousands of miles of cross-country ski trails. People also downhill ski at the famous Whistler-Blackcomb ski resort.

Lakes and ponds are cleared off for skating. Kids pull long wooden sleds called **toboggans** up big hills. Snow stings their cold cheeks as they ride back down. Canadians also enjoy ice hockey and snowmobiling.

There are also many summer outdoor activities. There are thousands of lakes and rivers to swim in, fish, sail, and explore. You can golf, play tennis, or hike. Along the ocean, you can scuba dive or whale-watch. Canada's land is so large that you will never run out of new things to do or see.

These people are canoeing in Banff National Park, Alberta, Canada.

Glossary

Ancestors: a person's family from long ago.

Canadians: citizens of Canada.

Europeans: people from Europe.

Fjords: a narrow section of sea between cliffs.

Gondola: a car that hangs from a cable, used to transport people.

Inuits: also called Eskimos, the native people who crossed over from Asia to North America more than 20,000 years ago.

Migration: the trips made by animals to find better places to eat and breed.

Native: the people who were first living on a specific part of land.

Prospectors: miners looking for gold.

Toboggans: long, wooden sleds.

Tundra: treeless area in the far North.

Undeveloped: not built on or farmed; land that is left alone.

Internet Sites

Canadian CultureNet
http://www.culturenet.ucalgary.ca/
CultureNet is a World Wide Web window on Canadian culture. It is a home for Canadian cultural networks.

The Disney World Explorer
http://www.disney.com/DisneyInteractive/WDWExplorer/
This is a fun and colorful site with trivia games, maps, previews, downloads, CD-ROM helpers and much, much more.

Grand Canyon Association
http://www.thecanyon.com/gca/
You're just a click away from a backpacking trip, a chance to meet canyon lovers like you, and books on this great region. This site has some great artwork.

Mexconnect
http://www.mexconnect.com/
This site has great travel ideas, Mexican art, tradition, food, history, and much more. It includes a chat room, tour section, and photo gallery.

Fantastic Journeys Yellowstone
http://www.nationalgeographic.com/features/97/yellowstone/index.html
Explore Yellowstone National Park, a place like no other on Earth. See strange marvels, go underground to find what causes them, and trigger an eruption of the famous geyser Old Faithful. A very cool site!

Marine Watch
http://www.marinewatch.com/
Welcome to Marine Watch, the international news journal about events occurring on, under and over the oceans of the planet. This site has many links and cool photos!

These sites are subject to change.

Pass It On

Adventure Enthusiasts: Tell us about places you've been or want to see. A national park, amusement park, or any exciting place you want to tell us about. We want to hear from you!

To get posted on the ABDO Publishing Company website E-mail us at
"Adventure@abdopub.com"
Visit the ABDO Publishing Company website at www.abdopub.com

Index

A

Alberta 8
ancestors 6
animals 8, 15
arctic 14

B

Banff National Park 8
British Columbia 6, 18

C

cities 4

D

dogsled 18

E

Eskimos 6
Europeans 6

F

festivals 4
food 10
French 10

G

gold 16

H

hockey 20
Hudson Bay 14

I

Inuits 6

J

Jasper National Park 8

K

Klondike River 16
Ksan Native Village 6

L

lakes 4, 8, 18, 20

M

Manitoba 12, 14
money 12
Montreal 4
mountains 4, 8
Mounties 10
museums 4, 6, 10

N

native 4, 6
North Pole 4
Nova Scotia 10

P

parks 4, 8
polar bears 14, 15
provinces 4

Q

Quebec 4, 10

R

Rocky Mountains 8
Royal Canadian Mint 12

S

Saskatchewan 10
ski trails 20
snowmobiling 20
sports 20
summer 20

T

territories 4
tundra 8, 14

V

Vancouver 4

W

whales 14
wilderness 16
wildlife 8
winter 20

Y

Yukon Territory 16